AF351598

In Praise of
the Lady of Power:

An English-Language Booklet of Prayers
Dedicated to La Santa Muerte

Rev. Anna Applegate

Nemetona Press, Gurnee, Illinois

First published March 2024 by Rev. Anna Applegate.
All rights reserved.

No part of this book may be reproduced, stored in a retrieval system, or transmitted in any form or by any means, including electronic, mechanical, photocopying, microfilming, recording, or otherwise, without written permission from the author.

All text is copyrighted.

Text copyright ©2024 by Rev. Anna Applegate.

All photographs of the various La Santa Muerte statues and altars portrayed herein are ©Rev. Anna Applegate.

Designed and typeset by Lost Dolly Graphics. Typeset in Adobe Anth and Garamond Pro.

ISBN 979-8-218-38918-5

Library of Congress Cataloging-in-Publication Data available upon request.

Acknowledgments

I'm indebted to my second Wasband for procuring for me a La Santa Muerte *Roja* statue from a wonderful Albuquerque, New Mexico, palace of retail enchantment known as *Masks y Màs* in 2013. That statue served as the gateway to my first direct encounter with the Bony Lady and my devotional practice exponentially grew from there. Thank you, Dan, and believe it or not I truly do wish you well in life. Blessings.

I'm grateful to Ken Kwilosz at Alchemy Arts Bookstore in Chicago for permitting me to host on-site public *misas*/spiritual masses dedicated to La Santa Muerte. Those have been among my most favorite experiences of group worship in my life.

I also want to thank Margie Higa-Funai of Honolulu, Hawaii, for her emotional support and for truly embodying *aloha* to a *malihini* (foreigner) like me throughout my duration of living on her peoples' magical island. I'm also very grateful for her serving as my first professional Tarot client. *Mahalo nui loa!*

I owe huge thanks and many a martini to the amazingly talented and equally skull motif-obsessed Cole of Lost Dolly Graphics for her invaluable help with the book design, and, more importantly, her loyal friendship over the past 14 years and counting. And I'm even grateful for the bizarre, subterranean *Office Space*-esque advertising job environment wherein we met and became giggling, Goth eyeliner-flaunting coworkers/sisters of another mother at together. Cheers to you, love!

Dedication

I dedicate this book to the memory of my late father Uroš and my late brother, Mark. *Večnaja Pamjat* / Memory Eternal.

I also dedicate this book to my *boricua* mentor/*madrina* in *Espiritismo*, Doña Julí, for calling down the spirits to confirm many things about myself and my life path that I always suspected were the case. I also owe my deepest thanks to Babalawo Jim, who introduced me to Julí, and to Babalawo Tito for furnishing me with Ifá's invaluable counsel for nearly two decades and counting. *Ashé!*

Last but certainly not least, I dedicate this book to the profound Mystery that is La Santa Muerte. *Viva La Dama Poderosa!* May Her devotees' numbers around the world continue to grow.

Table of Contents

Introduction

WHY THIS BOOK AND WHY NOW?

As of the commencement of this book's manuscript a little over a week into the new year of 2024, my north suburban Chicago home lies enveloped in winter's vise grip. The season serves as a powerful reminder to turn our thoughts not just toward the remembrances of our beloved dead and those who have gone before us, but towards our own inevitable mortality as well.

The Deities and spirits Who command end-of-life processes knock a little more loudly on our thick skulls, reminding us that our earthly lives are for a limited time only; tomorrow is promised to no mortal.

People have responded to these *memento mori* messages in a variety of ways across cultures and across the centuries. For me, as a contemporary Polytheist, legally ordained Pagan priestess, certified Death Midwife, and practicing Witch, I have always had an inner GPS orienting me towards Gods and spirits of death, the underworld, and the afterlife. Besides La Santa Muerte, I'm devoted to several Holy Powers associated with death and the underworld, from the Greek Hekate Khthonia, to the Norse Hel, to the Egyptian/Kemetic Nephthys and Her Son, Anubis, to my ancestral Slavic god, Veles.

My personal practices bear out something I've been witnessing in the broader Pagan "community" (or, more accurately, a series of related communities) for many years now: an intersectionality between devotional practices honoring various Deities and spirits with folkloric witchcraft tied to specific cultures and even landscapes, including spiritual landscapes or what I call "soulscapes."

With the "cult" of La Santa Muerte skyrocketing in popularity north of Mexico's border with the U.S., we have a set of beliefs and practices originally contextualized within Mexican folk Catholicism transgressing boundaries of all kinds, geographic as well as ideological, as more people of widely diverging backgrounds come to embrace with fervent devotion the notion of appealing to *La Dama Poderosa* ("the Powerful Lady") to help them navigate life's challenges.

MY HISTORY WITH LA SANTA MUERTE

Ever since early childhood, I've always loved images of the Grim Reaper and the Blue Öyster Cult song, "Don't Fear the Reaper." Thoughts of that mysterious, robed Figure holding a scythe, ready to mow us down at any second, excited me. I was very aware of the reality of death—I'd experienced several deaths in my family by the time I was eight years old—and I intellectually and emotionally accepted the reality of my own mortality. I was quite comfortable with the idea of having my little life end, of being buried and having my flesh rot (I was against the idea of embalming) and hopefully, I thought, I would be able to have my spirit merge into that of a tree, not unlike what happens to suicides in Dante Alighieri's medieval vision of *Limbo: The Forest of Suicides* as described in *The Inferno*.

But it wasn't until I was in my late twenties, at the turn of this millennium, that I first discovered La Santa Muerte, and the intrigue was immediate: a *female* Grim Reaper from Mexico! A Virgin Death Goddess! What are Her origins, I wondered—is She a modern incarnation of an ancient Aztec Death Goddess? Or a syncretic Being like the saints revered in Haitian Vodoun? *How do I approach Her?*

A Chicago native, I was raised in the Eastern Orthodox Church and my Serbian immigrant parents had my brother and me educated in Chicago Catholic schools our entire lives. As I began learning about La Santa Muerte, I was immediately struck by a weird energetic resonance of Hers that definitely reminded me of the Virgin Mary. The Most Holy Death is a powerful protector and a compassionate listener: maternal and loving, yes, but definitely fierce, unlike Mary, when She needs to be.

How do I begin praying to Her? What do I do?

My first procured image of La Santa Muerte was a relatively small statue depicting Her in Her "robe" or aspect of *La Roja*—the Lady of Love and Passion. I bought it in 2003 at my favorite occult bookstore in the city, Alchemy Arts, which I'd been patronizing since I was in high school in the late 80s to early 90s.

I instinctively lit candles and prayed before the statue. The goal was to effect a two-way relationship, but I still stumbled about, not sure where to receive guidance on giving offerings or doing any other cultic practices. There were zero books available, whether in Spanish or English, in the shops and *botanicas* I frequented. All I could find were the occasional glass five-day candles (red- or white-colored wax only) with a bilingual, all-purpose prayer to La Santa Muerte on the reverse.

Fast forward exactly ten years later, the year 2013, and my research began to involve long-sought personal guidance from Latinx folks I met in my House of Ifá, including psychic mediums, divination specialists, and Santeras who encouraged me to cultivate a devotional relationship with the Bony Lady. My relationship with Her fully commenced with devotional prayer services, which I perform on Mondays (for road-opening power) and Saturdays (the day to honor the dead).

My practices grew exponentially in November that year as a direct
result of my then-boyfriend gifting me with a large, wonderfully
handmade Mexican statue of La Santa Muerte *Roja*, which he bought
for me when he visited a marvelous shop called *Masks y Màs* in
Albuquerque, New Mexico. And at the time, it was our shared love
for the phenomenal TV series *Breaking Bad* that inspired him to buy
the statue for me! (If you're a fan of the show, you'll never forget
the impeccably dressed Salamanca twins and their debut in season
three when they set out on a pilgrimage to a La Santa Muerte shrine
somewhere in the deserts of Michoacán. How I loved those *brujo* bros!)

I set up a new shrine to La Santa Muerte in my bedroom the night I was
given the *La Roja* staue. I subsequently had a dream wherein She "told"
me (via telepathic communication) that She didn't want Her shrine
to be on the north wall of my bedroom, but to place Her in the south!
Upon awakening, I moved Her shrine and did a spontaneous ritual,
apologizing to Her for sticking Her in the north without consulting with
Her first; I heaped Her altar with lots of extra offerings of pieces of dark
chocolate, hoping She'd forgive my gaffe.

I knew somehow that She heard me and that She accepted my heartfelt
apology. From then on, I've had nothing but a sense of profound
contact every time I pray to Her.

THE EXPLOSIVE GLOBAL GROWTH
IN HER POPULARITY

As mentioned previously, the "cult" of La Santa Muerte as a postmodern
North- and Central-American religious phenomenon historically has
been contextualized within folk Catholicism; in fact, the majority of
La Santa Muerte's devotees in Mexico consider themselves to be good
practicing Catholics (Chestnut 80, 115).

Immediately, though, we know we've entered into non-canonical (from
the Catholic perspective) status due to the unique iconography La Santa
Muerte presents. We're not beholding the image of a flesh-and-blood
person but a striking image of a scythe-bearing skeleton, which would
be androgynous on its own, but now deliberately gendered female.
She's intimidating-looking to many. She's uncompromisingly powerful.
Yet, for Her devotees, She inspires such affectionate devotion, which is
demonstrated through cute epithets such as *La Niña Bonita* ("the Pretty
Girl") or *La Flaquíta* ("the Skinny Girl").

In Mexico, La Santa Muerte is the fastest growing folk "saint," almost on
par with the widely venerated saints of San Judas Tadeo or La Virgen de
Guadalupe (Chestnut 9).

Glass candles in a variety of wax colors (the color correspondences are important, as they translate to the "robes" La Santa Muerte wears, indicating the sphere of influence She can be petitioned for) bearing Her image and featuring bilingual prayers in Spanish and English can now routinely be found in virtually every grocery store that features a Latinx/Hispanic food section here in the United States, shelved next to candles depicting familiar (and canonical) Roman Catholic saints venerated throughout the Americas, such as San Martin Caballero or Santo Niño de Atocha (Chestnut 11).

But that's not to say the popularity of La Santa Muerte isn't being challenged, however. There is fierce resistance in some circles (Chestnut 12, 189). In fact, the Roman Catholic Church and evangelical Protestant churches are actively campaigning in Mexico to denounce the cult of La Santa Muerte as, predictably, not just heretical but "Satanic," sensationalizing Her worship in true yellow journalism tradition and tarnishing Her legions of devotees who, incidentally, come from all walks of life (Chestnut 11) as murderous drug traffickers engaged in lurid, immoral, and downright criminal rituals replete with human sacrifice (Chestnut 10, 113).

The degree of vitriol is astounding. Clearly, the cult of La Santa Muerte is perceived as a threat to the institutions (ecclesiastical and civil) committed to upholding the status quo. Could it be because Death personified, not unlike the Hindu Goddess Kali-Ma, is a liberator? First and foremost, La Santa Muerte offers Her devotees freedom from the fear of death; a close second is freedom from judgment: Unlike the canonical saints within Catholicism, La Santa Muerte *never* frowns upon or denies any petitioner's request from a moral high horse stance. Hers is a morally ambivalent universe (Chestnut 193).

This is the reason why both criminals and members of law enforcement/the military in Mexico invoke Her for aid in their daily work (Chestnut 19, 108). When La Santa Muerte *Negra* (the Lady in Black) casts Her cloak over Her devotees, it is thought that they receive Her blessing of physical and spiritual protection via invisibility magic. Whether that invisibility translates into traveling undetected on foot in a notoriously unsafe *barrio* of Mexico City to prevent getting robbed or abducted, or because a cartel is shipping kilos of illegal narcotics across the Mexico-U.S. border and they don't want the prying eyes of the law to see their "precious cargo," it is believed that *La Negrita* will conceal such petitions underneath Her cloak of darkness and help those who wish to avoid discovery fly under the radar.

Again, La Santa Muerte doesn't judge people for their desires, including sexual ones, which means She is perhaps *the* Patron Goddess of the LGBTQ+ community (Prower 14). How citizens behave, their willingness or lack thereof to uphold the laws decreed in a civil society—She's not judging anyone for any of it because She knows everyone, regardless of economic power or race or gender expression or social standing, will someday fall to Her scythe. As mere mortals, we can petition Her that our deaths be good ones.

Another major reason why people are drawn to Her cult is that many folks from Christian backgrounds, in desperation, tried praying first to Jesus or to various canonical saints for help in their dire situations, only to have those prayers go unanswered. Feeling rebuffed, they subsequently turned their attention to the skeletal grin of *La Santísima*, and then they experienced profound epiphanies when it was clear that She answered their prayers (Prower 15). Incidentally, She is known for quick turn-around time in answering prayers (Chestnut 59, 192). She has found many champions from the ranks of the working poor, the marginalized, even the incarcerated—those who in some way or another would find themselves drowning in the mainstream without Her help (Rollin 20).

IN LIVING COLOR: THE ROBES OF LA SANTA MUERTE

La Santa Muerte has various aspects based on color correspondences, but the three most popular are also, interestingly, the colors of the Goddess of Fate as taught in Traditional European Witchcraft circles: red, black, and white. La Santa Muerte *Roja* is Whom we turn to for the affairs of the heart, whether that means attracting a new lover, keeping the one you've got, or having a straying lover return to you. She appeals to everyone, regardless of sexual orientation.

La Santa Muerte *Negra* is prayed to for protection and concealment, as well as magical offense (i.e., hexing) and acts of vengeance.

La Santa Muerta *Blanca* affords magical defense and the safeguarding of innocence and purity, physical as well as energetic—this is the "virgin" archetype in our modern sense that connotes "purity" and being "untainted" by sexual energies.

La Santa Muerte *Azul* can have different interpretations depending on where in the U.S. you are. In my part of the Midwest, She is the blue-mantled Lady of Healing, granting freedom from physical and mental maladies as well as the crippling effects of addiction. However, in the Southwest, such as what I experienced in a prayer service at a *botanica* in San Antonio, Texas, in 2021, She is prayed to in a "Law Stay Away" *(Contra La Ley)* capacity. My prayer to Her in this book is expressly for the former. The Blue-Robed Skinny Lady is also supposed to be the Robe students pray to for help with their studies (Rollin 185).

La Dorada has a gold-colored robe, though She is sometimes adorned in a robe of dollar bills for wealth. She can also appear in the robe of *Tres Metales*—copper, gold, and silver—showcasing the treasures mined from the earth. We pray to Her for wealth and steady work.

One of my favorites is La Santa Muerte *Verde*—the Green-Robed *Santísima* of Justice. You appeal to Her for justice both personal and collective, from winning a court case or settling other legal disputes in your favor to upholding Cosmic Order (Chestnut 69). In that latter sense, She is very much on the same frequency as the Egyptian Goddess *Ma'at* to me.

La Morada, the Purple-Robed Santa Muerte, is invoked for communion with the Divine, for activating and reinforcing your Higher Self, and for strengthening your receptivity to psychic states. Think along the New Age parameter of "crown chakra activation." However, She is not to be confused with the Brown-Robed *(La Marróna)* La Santa Muerte, Who is *La Santísima* of Necromancy, summoning the dead.

There's even a *Seven-Colored/Rainbow-hued* La Santa Muerte to cover all of your bases in terms of petitions, or for requesting Her aid in a crisis on multiple fronts (Chestnut 199-200). Naturally, this aspect is widely venerated by Her Queer devotees.

The iconography of La Santa Muerte is constant, no matter which colored "robe" She's wearing. She carries Her scythe in one skeletal hand and a globe in the other, for no mortal on the planet can escape Death. She also carries Her scales of Judgment (especially *La Verde*). She typically has an owl draped on Her Person or perched before Her. If She's depicted enthroned, the owl dutifully perches on an arm rest, yellow eyes gleaming forward. *La Niña Hermosa* sees through the gloom of the underworld with owl-like vision, navigating the dark with ease.

In many cultures, owls have the dual connotations of wisdom and death. Also, witches in countries as diverse as Zimbabwe, Italy, and the Federated States of Micronesia are said to disguise themselves as owls in order to unobtrusively carry out the workings of their Craft at night.

No matter which aspect of La Santa Muerte one decides to petition with prayer, it's universally agreed upon that She is demanding and She needs Her own shrine. This was emphasized to me by my *Espiritismo* godmother.

Do NOT place images of La Santa Muerte adjacent to statues of other saints if you're Catholic or other Deities, even fellow Death Deities, if you're a Polytheist. She won't like it, and She may express Her displeasure in costly ways. (It *is* okay to place images or statues of Her depicted in one robe next to images of Her in other-colored robes, though. My own altar photos throughout this book bear this out.)

OFFERINGS TO LA SANTA MUERTE

Offerings to La Santa Muerte include candy, expensive chocolates, cigarettes/tobacco/marijuana blunts (the smoke of any of these herbals are blown directly onto Her statues' faces), fresh flowers (dispose of them right away when they show signs of wilting), fruit (red apples, oranges, papayas, bananas), sheaves of wheat (She's a Reaper) or whole wheat bread or white bread rolls you can get in a Mexican bakery/*panaderia* called *bolillo* (Chestnut 78). Dispose of food by the third day, says my *Espiritismo* godmother.

In addition to whichever kind of liquor you decide to offer Her—ranging from beer to tequila to red wine—She also has to have a glass of water on Her shrine, one that is refreshed daily. It's said that She gets very thirsty for water because of all the traveling She does around the world to answer peoples' prayers (Chestnut 72).

Given Her association with owls mentioned above, if you can find any figurines or other objects depicting owls that are able to fit on your altar space, She'd appreciate it. I made a turquoise beaded bracelet with a large owl charm on it as a devotional offering to La Santa Muerte Verde and the statue I have "wears" the bracelet.

No doubt about it: La Santa Muerte is unapologetically powerful. But I also find a delightful childlike quality to Her; in my devotionals, I feel Her take great pleasure in Her offerings with a pure innocence akin to a child expressing great delight at being given a favorite treat. I think it's that very childlike quality to Her that inspires such affection on the part of devotees of all ages: images of La Santa Muerte are lovingly carried about in public on Mexican streets, especially when the *Día de Muertos* festivals get underway in Mexico City and elsewhere. The scene is reminiscent of children holding aloft beloved, living dolls.

You can see examples of this in the footage of a short documentary film CNN produced in 2017 called *Spiritually Curious Believer with Reza Aslan;* Google it, it's worth the watch. Mr. Aslan purchased a La Santa Muerte Negra statue in Mexico City and holding the statue for the first time, he declared that he felt like he was "holding his own living child." Even he was surprised by the level of affection he was feeling for his La Santa Muerte statue, which definitely had a living presence to it. He found his day of participation in an outdoor Mass to La Santa Muerte to be deeply moving.

That's the kind of effect She has on people.

A WORD ABOUT THE PRAYERS THAT FOLLOW

For the most part, devotional rituals to La Santa Muerte are contextualized within wider Roman Catholic or Catholic-inspired liturgy (Chestnut 192), so that's kind of the format I chose for my prayers. I'm not "pushing" Catholicism or Abrahamic religious sensibilities on anyone—I'm certainly not a monotheist myself—just trying to set these prayers in their Mexican cultural context, and Mexico is an overwhelmingly Catholic country, excursions by militant evangelical Protestants in the past 20 years notwithstanding.

If you can get your hands on Spanish-language Mexican prayer books, you'll often find that prayers to La Santa Muerte are "sealed" by a threefold repetition of either "The Hail Mary," "The Lord's Prayer/Our Father," or "The Glory Be" prayers, and I've included some of those traditional Catholic forms of closure with some of these prayers. If you were raised Catholic and you know these prayers and you don't have any objection to reciting them, then please recite them joyfully. If you don't want to pray those prayers and just want to address La Santa Muerte on Her own without the Catholic "trappings," that's fine as well.

Some of the prayers have a call-and-response format—especially when petitions are being offered—and they thus lend themselves well to group recitation. I'd encourage anyone to get a spiritually compatible group of friends together to recite the prayers in unison, which can be an extremely effective way of raising energy to "feed" La Santa Muerte in addition to the tangible offerings given to Her of fruit, candy, flowers, water, alcohol, etc.

It is my profound hope with the publication of this little book that She will touch readers' hearts as profoundly as She's touched mine. This book is an act of devotion: an offering in itself to La Santa Muerte. May She be ever praised!

Prayers to the Various Robes of *La Santísima*

INVOCATION/PRAYER OF THE MOST HOLY DEATH
(To be said at the outset of any prayers to any of Her robes;
adapted from a traditional Mexican prayer)

Lord, before Your Divine Presence, God Almighty,
Father, Son, and Holy Spirit,
I ask for Your permission to invoke the Holy Death, *Oh Pretty Girl!*
La Niña Hermosa, I want to humbly ask that You break and destroy
All harmful spells and dark intentions of others
That may present themselves
Before my person, in my home, and on my path.
Holy Death, please relieve me of all oppression, poverty, and despair.
I ask that You please grant me ________________.
Enlighten, with Your Holy Presence, my home, my workplace,
And the environments of my loved ones.
Award us health, love, prosperity, and well-being.
Blessed and praised be Your charity, Holy Death.
Lord, I give You infinite thanks because I see Your charity.
The challenges I face every day are perfecting my spirit.
La Santísima, I give You thanks because in the midst of these challenges
I always have Your Holy Blessing.
Amen.

PRAYERS ADDRESSED TO *LA BLANCA*/THE WHITE ROBE OF *LA SANTÍSIMA*

Prayer to La Santa Muerte *Blanca* for Protection

Dear Death of my Heart,
Never leave me unprotected.
With Your powerful left hand,
Sweep away and cut down with Your scythe
All treacherous obstacles
Standing in the way of my fulfillment of my destiny.
Mow down all my enemies.
Cut the ropes to the snares they lay out for me;
I shall not be caught in their traps.
With Your powerful right hand,
Cast Your cloak of Protection about me:
Safeguarding me, in Your Brilliant Light,
Against all foes, physical and spiritual,
Visible and invisible.
Luz! Luz! Luz!
I stand strong in Your Light,
La Dama Poderosa.
This is the Divine Virtue
God has granted You.
In God I believe, but in You I trust.

(Close with reciting "The Lord's Prayer" three times.)

Second Prayer for Protection

Most Holy Death,
Glorious and Powerful
Sister of Mercy,
Stand firm as my Protector,
My unwavering shield
Against all foes,
Those known and those not known to me.
Be my guiding light
When all avenues seem dark,
Ensuring the safety of my body and
The wellness of my mind and spirit.
Lady of Purity,
Lady of Righteousness,
Seated at the Right Hand of the Father,
May I always find refuge in
Your mantle of Protection,
Granting me spiritual and physical
Protection and peace.
So shall it be.

("Seal" this prayer by reciting the "Hail Mary" three times.)

Prayer for Protection Before Travel

(Note: The night before your trip begins, light a yellow seven-day glass candle.)

Holy Death,
I invoke Your Holy Name to ask that You
Make an easy path for me through the skies, the roads,
The seas, and the rivers.
See me safely across valleys and mountains.
Never cease to bring me Your good fortune.
Shelter me within Your cloak, granting me Your powerful protection,
Neutralizing any misfortune that might come my way.
Do not let simple problems escalate into larger ones.
I beg of You, Holy Death, Merciful Lady,
Help me avoid accidents, illness, and delays;
Keep away all tragedy, pain, and lack.
I light this candle for You.
Let its light form a protective wall around me.
Give me patience and understanding among strangers.
Please, Lady of the Shadows, grant me strength, power, and wisdom.
Allow the Elements to stay Their wrath upon my path.
Help me to return home happy and peaceful,
So that I may adore and praise You at Your holy shrine.

(Follow with recitations of "The Lord's Prayer" three times. Upon returning from your trip, light a white seven-day glass candle in appreciation.)

Dream Incubation Prayer

I invoke Your Presence, Holy Lady Death.
Stir from Your dark world.
I humbly ask You for Your advice:
Speak into my left ear and let me know what to do.
The horizon before me is uncertain
And the future fearful.
Cast Your mantle of protection about me,
My Sweet Lady,
And give me Your advice.
Let my dreams reveal unambiguous signs
That I may clearly receive Your message.
I patiently await Your answer,
Giving You thanks and praise.
Amen.

PRAYERS ADDRESSED TO *LA ROJA* / THE RED ROBE OF *LA SANTÍSIMA*

Prayer of Adoration (Bilingual) to La Santa Muerte *Roja*

Oh, La Santa Muerte Roja!
Yo te venero!
Yo te saludo,
La Dama Mucha Felicidad y Amor!
Blessed Rose of Life,
Your blooming season blesses me with love
And I give great thanks!
From the dawn of my life to its sunset,
I bask in Your vital force of unending love
And I give great thanks!
For the warmth of lovers past and present,
I give great thanks!
For the rosy pleasures of life
And the kindling of my inner fire,
I give great thanks!
For the love I radiate within myself for my Self and for others,
I give great thanks!
Bonita La Roja,
Lady Who makes life worth living,
May You be ever hailed!
Viva La Santísima!

Petition to La Santa Muerte *Roja* for a New Lover

Oh, Mi Flaquíta!
Scarlet-robed bestower of sensual delights!
You Who nourish body and spirit alike,
Hear my heartfelt plea:
Draw unto me a lover who resonates with my heart's own song,
The frequencies of respect and integrity,
Of playful exploration,
Of unbridled ecstasy!
Lady of the Red Thread,
I trust that You will weave
The right connections for me
With the right partner
At the appointed time.
My desire proposes but it is You Who disposes!
Amen.

PRAYERS ADDRESSED TO *LA NEGRA*/THE BLACK ROBE OF *LA SANTÍSIMA*

Petition of Victory: Antiphonal Chant
(Adapted from a traditional Mexican prayer)

RITUAL LEADER: You Who became immortal after conquering the world
And overcoming difficulties with All-Knowing Wisdom,

ALL: Please, Sacred Death, let me always be a victor in this world.

RITUAL LEADER: For all the agony and pain You give to the dying
In their final seconds of living in this world,

ALL: Please, Sacred Death, let me always be a victor in this world.

RITUAL LEADER: For all the emotions that You release
When a soul is leaving this plane,

ALL: Please, Sacred Death, let me always be a victor in this world.

RITUAL LEADER: As we await the joyful reunion with our loved ones
No longer living in this world,

ALL: Please, Sacred Death, let me always be a victor in this world.

RITUAL LEADER: It is of essential importance to be brave as we face life,
That we fear nothing and that nothing can stop us
Nor we cease of loving You in any way.

ALL: Please, Sacred Death, let me always be a victor in this world.

RITUAL LEADER: In the Name of Our Lord and Savior, Jesus Christ.

ALL: Amen.

"Return to Sender" Prayer to *La Negra*
(Adapted from a traditional Mexican prayer)

Lady Death,
Skeletal Spirit,
Powerful, Strong, and Indispensable,
In moments of anguish
I invoke Your kindness,
Plead to God Almighty,
Concede what I am asking of You:
That whomever shall wish me harm
Shall repent for the rest of their lives.
Let the harm or the envy of their evil eyes
Return to them immediately.
May those who ignore Your command,
Feel Your Power,
Good Spirit Death!
While at leisure or in business,
I declare You my Advocate,
And everyone who comes against me,
Let them lose!
Oh Lady of Death, my Protecting Angel!

Prayer to *La Negra* to Slice Away Witchcraft of the Mouth

Most Holy Death,
I kneel at Your feet to implore You
To be my steadfast shield and guard against
The wagging tongues of the envious, the malicious, and the spiteful.
Do not let their evil intentions coalesce and rise up against me.
Rather, may Your protecting scythe slice through
The miasma of their words,
Rendering them powerless.
Mow down whatever obstacles and deceptions block the Truth,
For You clear all pathways.
My Lady, there is no evil that You cannot vanquish,
No injustice that You cannot redress,
No intractable situation that doesn't wither when met by
Your intercession.
I surrender myself to You.
Viva La Santísima!

VELADORA AROMATICA
MUERTE ORO
VELADORA

PRAYERS ADDRESSED TO *LA DORADA*/THE GOLD ROBE OF *LA SANTÍSIMA*

Prayer to *La Dorada* for Steady Work and Income

Oh Sovereign Lady!
My time in this life is short, departures sudden.
I plead with You,
My Holy Treasure in Life,
To grant me gainful and steady employment
That I may provide for myself
And my family
And never lack in the necessities of well-being.
Lady of Riches,
Open the doors to gainful employment!
Open the doors to good fortune!
Unleash prosperity to enter my home from all doors,
Allowing the cash flow to be more than enough
To cover all my needs.
With Your sharp scythe,
Mow down all adverse circumstances
That may afflict me.
Keep envy away,
And grant me contentment.
Amen.

Prayer to *La Dorada* for Financial Well-Being

La Santísima,
I will see You face to face sooner or later,
As You, without regard to age or riches,
Claim the old, the young, even the newly born
To come to Your feet at the appointed time.
Until that last day, hour, and second when
Your Divine Majesty commands me to appear at Your feet,
Grant unto me Your favor
That my life will be well lived:
Alleviate all financial insecurity, all poverty and despair,
Bringing instead the health and joy
That comes in the wake of steady work and self-worth.
Let my business endeavors, my bank accounts,
And everything I do to provide for my family flourish.
Blessed and praised be Your Generosity,
Holy Death.
In God I believe but in You I trust!
Amen.

Health Is Wealth Prayer to *La Dorada*

Holy and Virtuous Death,
Miraculous Lady of Majesty,
I humbly ask that You reinforce my
Health, the true source of my wealth.
Drive away all spirits of illness;
Keep me from falling into their traps.
Keep me from all harm
And spiritual malevolence.
Grant me luck, health, happiness, steady work, and money.
Help me to overcome every obstacle.
Sweep all illusions and delusions from my path.
Anything I desire,
Any foundation I hope to establish for my vocation,
Will help build a promising success with Your Holy Blessing.
This is the Divine Virtue God granted You.
In God I believe but in You I trust.

(Close with reciting "The Lord's Prayer" three times.)

PRAYER ADDRESSED TO *LA NIÑA AZUL*/ THE BLUE ROBE OF *LA SANTÍSIMA*

Prayer for Healing to *La Santa Muerte Azul*

Oh, La Dama Poderosa!
Mother of Might,
Mother of Mercy,
I ask for Your blue healing mantle
To enfold me
And bring me healing and peace.
From the storms of life,
I seek refuge in Your calm.
For the healing of my mind,
Your Wisdom gives me peace.
For the healing of my body,
Your Power gives me strength.
With the unwavering might
Of Your falling scythe,
I rejoice at the cutting of cords to
All substances, people, places, and events
That previously brought my body poison,
My emotions turmoil,
And my home unrest.
With one touch from Your bony fingers,
Well-being is restored.
La Niña Azul,
I give You thanks and praise.
Wellspring of Healing,
I give You thanks and praise.
Compassionate *La Santísima,*
I give You thanks and praise.
Amen.

PRAYER ADDRESSED TO *LA MARRÓNA*/THE BROWN ROBE OF *LA SANTÍSIMA*

Prayer to Begin a Sèance (Group)
or A Necromantic Working (Solo)

Oh, *La Marróna!*
Keeper of Mysteries as timeless and as pervasive
As the earth beneath my/our feet,
You Who breach the silence of the gaping grave
Destined to one day, by Your summons, become my/our own resting place,
Hear me/us, I/we humbly pray.
I have readied my mind / We have readied our minds
And this environment to speak with the spirits.
With my/our own courage and with confidence in Your Power,
Your Protection,
I/We ask that at this time that is not a time, in this place that is not a place,
You conjure the magic of the In-Between
So that a meeting place desirable to the spirits can form
In our shared realities and welcome them in.
By Your mighty scythe, *La Dama Poderosa,*
Motion for the spirit(s) I/we seek to communicate with to draw near.
Please bring unto me/us [NAME THE DEAD, IF KNOWN]
That I/we might speak with them and find comfort in their whispered words.
Shepherdess of the Dead, hear my/our prayer.
It is not to vex the dead that I/we awaken them through Your agency
And ask that they be delivered unto me/unto all who are gathered here,
But by Your mercy, the spirit(s), by consenting to speak with me/us,
Will further the cause of their own ongoing elevation into the Light.
Ashé!
Wise *La Marróna,* All-Powerful Spirit Summoner,
Open Your brown robe and let the spirits I/we wish to speak with come forth.
Let [NAME THE DEAD] enter into this sanctified place.
Open their mouths that they may speak clearly to me/us,
Ensuring clarity of communication.
Drive away all false spirits, tricksters masquerading
As the dearly departed, and parasitic entities.
They do not have my/our permission to enter this space!
Protect me/everyone gathered here from all spiritual danger.
And at the appointed time, O Queen of the Gibbering Dead,
Peacefully return [NAME THE DEAD] to their place of blessed repose,
And I/we will pray for their souls to be continually lifted up
Into Light and Grace.
May it be so!

(Ring a small bell or clap hands loudly three times to "seal" the petition.)

PRAYERS ADDRESSED TO *LA VERDE*/THE GREEN ROBE OF *LA SANTÍSIMA*

Prayer for Legal Proceedings/Court Cases

La Dama Poderosa,
Lady of Righteousness,
Mother of Justice,
Wielder of the Scales of Cosmic Order,
Help me redress the wrongs that I have suffered at the hands of
[NAME LEGAL ADVERSARY/ADVERSARIES OR SITUATION].
Relieve me of my burdens and help me to claim justice in this matter.
You know that my heart weighs on the side of Truth.
Be my advocate in the Courts, both Celestial and Worldly,
So that the judge(s) will decide in my favor.
I ask that you relentlessly cut away all ensnarling entanglements,
All bureaucratic ineptitude,
All escalating financial costs, and
All stalling tactics from my adversary/adversaries,
Expediting the release of just judgment on my behalf.
Glorious *La Santa Muerte Verde,*
You Who see the Truth even in the midst of darkness,
Grant me victory without delay
And I will publicly praise You for nine days!*
Amen!

---

*It goes without saying that you had better keep whatever kind of promise you make to La Santa Muerte.

Petition for Stability of the Body Politic in a Time of Deepening Divisions

O, Holy Lady Death!
Mother of Might,
Mother of Mercy,
I humbly ask that You shine Your Lamp of Wisdom
And illuminate the minds and hearts
Of all elected officials in this land.
Remind them of who it is, exactly, that they are sworn to serve.
Instill courage into the hearts of all people who adore You
And are ready to receive Your counsel and Your aid.
Grant us freedom from fear of change.
Grant us freedom from fear of the "Other."
Grant us bravery when we are cast in the role of the "Other."
Grant us freedom from fear of death;
Let us squarely reckon with our frail mortality without denial or trepidation.
Let us rejoice at the appointed time when we are summoned before You.
We move freely in this world with ease,
Knowing that nothing can stop us
Nor keep us from loving You with all that we are and have.
Amen!

In Praise of the Mother of Eternal Justice

Holy and Virtuous Death,
Miraculous Lady of Majesty,
I give You thanks and praise!
You are the Mother of Eternal Justice,
Holding aloft the Scales of Cosmic Order.
You see into the hearts of the wicked and the good
Here on Earth,
And I ask that You continue to champion the weak and the vulnerable.
Protect them from corrupt judges, prison wardens, lawyers,
And anyone who commits perjury.
Strike down injustice in its myriad of manifestations
And the totality of its systemic oppression.
La Niña Bonita,
At the right time You will judge me and take all the words
I have ever pronounced
And all the deeds I have ever committed
As the measure of my punishment or my absolution.
En Dios creo, pero en Ti confío! (In God I believe, but in You I trust!)
Viva La Santísima!

PRAYERS ADDRESSED TO THE SEVEN-COLORED/ RAINBOW ROBE OF *LA SANTÍSIMA*

Daily Gratitude Prayer

Oh, *La Santísima*, gleaming bone-white beneath
Your dazzling, richly arrayed robe
Whose colors speak to the vibrancy and the beauty of the gift of life,
Both earthly and eternal,
I honor You.
To You I give my thanks and praise for the sheer joy of being alive.
To You I give my thanks and praise for the gifts of my senses
Housed in my very own body, which allows me
To fully experience this world
As my sovereign Self.
To You I give my thanks and praise for my questing mind and its ability
To discover new worlds and to be receptive to Your wisdom and guidance.
To You I give my thanks and praise for all the material blessings,
Those that already surround me and those that are on their way, *ashé,*
That lay the foundation for my life, health, and well-being.
To You I give my thanks and praise for all of the ways
That love uplifts me every day,
In the giving and sending of soul-nourishing, fear-breaking,
Heart-mending love.
May I be made a more perfect vessel of Your love
Every moment of every day and throughout the quiet hours of the night.
Love, blessed Love, expanding from the center of my being
And radiating outwards to all whom I meet.
It is my prayer that by meeting me, all people encounter You
And feel the loving Presence at the heart of Your Mysteries.
For both the living and the dead, Love is the Gateway to Your Truth.
Oh, *Mi Flaquíta,*
To You I give my thanks and praise for the opportunity to be here now
And marvel at the majesty of this perfectly created Universe, knowing
I play an important role in the beautiful unfolding of it all,
During my lifetime and beyond it, rejoicing that my spiritual essence
Is made up of and will continue to evolve into Light!
Luz! Luz! Luz!
Your Rainbow Robe is a powerful reminder of these and
Many other Truths, none of which I take for granted.
Your kaleidoscope of colors whirls into Infinity, as does my
Love for You and my deepest thanks for Who You are.
Viva La Santísima!

Prayer for the Protection of Queer and Trans Folks

Merciful Sister, *La Santísima,*
Adorned in Your Rainbow Robe that serves as a symbolic reminder to us all of
The *necessity,* as well as the beauty, of *diversity* in life,
In the natural world but especially in human societies,
Hear this prayer roaring from my unquiet heart.
Lay Your mantle of protection over me and my beloveds
In the Queer and Trans communities.
Empower us.
Lend us Your strength and come to our aid.
We are in dire need, *La Dama Poderosa!*
Make safe our pathways as we go about our daily lives;
Keep my loved ones and I, but especially all Trans youth everywhere,
Safe from physical harm and harassment of any kind,
Whether in person or online.
Drive far from our midst and politically overturn and disenfranchise
Those who would wish upon us violence and the elimination of our rights.
Do not let these hateful bigots set us back decades
In our hard-fought struggle for civil rights!
In Your Name, may there at last be Equality, Equity, and Inclusion for all,
The promise of this country's Bill of Rights fulfilled.
Give us the means to legislate our pain and our rage into
Effecting positive social change. Open our roads favorably.
Embolden our straight allies to not falter
In their support for our communities.
May the resources we need appear and multiply.
May the ranks of politically progressive voters of all ages keep expanding,
All of us united under the fold of Your multi-hued Robe, La Santa Muerte!
Please guide the members of my Tribe currently experiencing
Homelessness due to ostracism from their families into safe spaces.
Comfort the shunned. Shame the oppressors!
You Who hear the cries of those who are marginalized and dispossessed,
All those who are targeted for the "crime" of being *Other,*
Aid us, comfort us, empower us, and magnify our voices into one chorus
Whose clarion call for justice will not be denied!
For the harm of none and the good of all in the LGBTQ+ community and me,
So may it be!

CLOSING PRAYER

In Praise of the Holy Death

In the Name of the Father, and the Son, and the Holy Spirit,
Immaculate being of Light,
I implore that You grant me these favors that I ask of You.
Until the last day, hour, and second
When Your Divine Majesty *orders* me to come to Your feet,
Dear Death of My Heart,
Do not ever leave me unprotected.

(Close with reciting "The Lord's Prayer" three times.)

A Novena to La Santa Muerte

DAY ONE

In the Roman Catholic Church, November is the traditional month
for praying the Novena: a nine-day prayer devoted to the Holy Mother
or to a saint. Given, as mentioned previously, that the majority of
La Santa Muerte's devotees consider themselves practicing Catholics,
it's not surprising in the least that the Novena format has been adapted
for Her worship.

According to my *Espiritismo* godmother, a Novena should always begin
on a Tuesday. Adorn your shrine to La Santa Muerte with fresh flowers
and a glass of clear water. A shot glass with tequila, rum, or sugar cane
alcohol (don't be cheap; She likes the good stuff!) is always a good
idea as well, as are sweets, apples, and the type of bread roll known as
a *bolillo*. The Novena will additionally require three white three-day glass
candles (commonly available at a *botanica* or even the Hispanic/Latino
foods section of grocery stores). Burn incense—copal is traditional.

When you are ready, make the Sign of the Cross and say
the Invocation/Prayer of the Most Holy Death.

INVOCATION/PRAYER OF THE MOST HOLY DEATH

Lord, before Your Divine Presence, God Almighty,
Father, Son, and Holy Spirit,
I ask for Your permission to invoke the Holy Death, *Oh Pretty Girl!*
La Niña Hermosa, I want to humbly ask that You break and destroy
All harmful spells and dark intentions of others
That may present themselves
Before my person, in my home, and on my path.
Holy Death, please relieve me of all oppression, poverty, and despair.
I ask that You please grant me ______________.
Enlighten, with Your Holy Presence, my home, my workplace,
And the environments of my loved ones.
Award us health, love, prosperity, and well-being.
Blessed and praised be Your charity, Holy Death.
Lord, I give You infinite thanks because I see Your charity.
The challenges I face every day are perfecting my spirit.
La Santísima, I give You thanks because in the midst of these challenges
I always have Your Holy Blessing.
Amen.

Now light the white candle to last for the next three days and pray the Novena prayer for the first day:

Oh, Holy Death!
The favors that I ask of You will help me overcome any difficulty.
With Your aid, nothing is impossible.
No obstacles will block my path,
And I will not fall into the snares laid for me by my enemies.
You safeguard me from all harm, my Protector!
Let only true friends with my best interests at heart cross my path.
Let my career, and everything I do, flourish.
May abundance overflow in my household,
Wrapped under Your protective mantle.

Now pray "The Lord's Prayer" three times.

Conclude with the Closing Prayer.

CLOSING PRAYER

In Praise of the Holy Death

In the Name of the Father, and the Son, and the Holy Spirit,
Immaculate being of Light,
I implore that You grant me these favors that I ask of You.
Until the last day, hour, and second
When Your Divine Majesty *orders* me to come to Your feet,
Dear Death of My Heart,
Do not ever leave me unprotected.

DAY TWO

For the second day of the Novena to La Santa Muerte, which should be a Wednesday, study how the white three-day candle you lit the previous day is burning. Is the glass clear or smoky at its top edges? That can indicate Divine favor or the withholding of it (or challenges to the manifestation of your prayers). How is the flame behaving? If it's active, flickering and making little crackling sounds, *La Santísima* is busy at work on your behalf. A slow but steady burn is fine, too.

Dump out the stale water in Her clear glass from the previous day and offer fresh water, same thing with the tequila. If the *bolillo* bread roll has hardened overnight, swap it out with a fresh one. (Never throw bread in the garbage; I always crumble mine up and feed it to birds.) Cookies and candies from the previous day are still good to retain on the altar, as are the flowers. Pro tip: chrysanthemums are traditional flowers for the dead in Mexican culture and they're hardy and long-lasting, making them ideal flowers to offer to La Santa Muerte.

The second day of the Novena introduces a prayer that is illustrative of the "command and control" magic that is a staple of La Santa Muerte's *cultus*. If someone has wronged you, or if a lover's commitment to you seems dubious, feel free to add three drops of "Holy Death" oil, "Adam & Eve" oil, or "Do As I Say" oil to recalibrate any imbalance. Petitions to redress injustice are best addressed to La Santa Muerte Verde.

Just as with the previous day, when you're ready to begin, make the Sign of the Cross and say the Prayer of the Most Holy Death.

INVOCATION/PRAYER OF THE MOST HOLY DEATH

Lord, before Your Divine Presence, God Almighty,
Father, Son, and Holy Spirit,
I ask for Your permission to invoke the Holy Death, *Oh Pretty Girl!*
La Niña Hermosa, I want to humbly ask that You break and destroy
All harmful spells and dark intentions of others
That may present themselves
Before my person, in my home, and on my path.
Holy Death, please relieve me of all oppression, poverty, and despair.
I ask that You please grant me ________________.
Enlighten, with Your Holy Presence, my home, my workplace,
And the environments of my loved ones.
Award us health, love, prosperity, and well-being.
Blessed and praised be Your charity, Holy Death.
Lord, I give You infinite thanks because I see Your charity.

The challenges I face every day are perfecting my spirit.
La Santísima, I give You thanks because in the midst of these challenges
I always have Your Holy Blessing.
Amen.

If you need to add your drops of essential oils to the already burning
candle, do it now. Then pray the Novena prayer for the second day:

Holy Death,
My Great Treasure,
You ate Your bread and kindly offered me a piece.
Gracious Hostess, Mighty in the Mansion of Life,
Allow me to walk victoriously in the short time allotted to me in this world.
Grant me this favor:
That [NAME], who did me wrong,
Is subject to the immutable weighing of Your Scales.
Let not their† wicked deeds escape Your attention!
Bring [NAME] to my feet, humbled and remorseful.
See to it that they never leave my side as long as it pleases me.
Let [NAME] fulfill the promise that was made to me.
And if [NAME] ignores Your command,
Then let [NAME] experience the weight of Your Judgment
On their head and
Feel Your Power, Good Spirit Death!
I declare You my Advocate, *Mi Flaquíta,*
And I rejoice that no force can make me cease loving You.
Your mercy is my greatest blessing.

Again, follow with "The Lord's Prayer" three times.

As you did the previous day, conclude with the Closing Prayer.

CLOSING PRAYER

In Praise of the Holy Death

In the Name of the Father, and the Son, and the Holy Spirit,
Immaculate being of Light,
I implore that You grant me these favors that I ask of You.
Until the last day, hour, and second
When Your Divine Majesty *orders* me to come to Your feet,
Dear Death of My Heart,
Do not ever leave me unprotected.

† I'm using "they/them/their" third-person pronouns in a first-person context. I know it's not
technically grammatically correct, but it's inclusive, and I don't want to encumber the sentences
of the prayers with the clunky "she/he/they" format instead each and every time!

DAY THREE

This third day, a Thursday, should be the day that you light the second in your trio of three-day glass candles with white wax. If at all possible, transfer, using a stick of incense or the head of a match, the flame from the first candle before it expires to the second one. As you do so, say:

"Flame to flame, the purity of my intentions is ignited."

If the first candle has already burned out, don't worry about it. Dress the second candle with any essential oils or herbs that would correspond with your intentions. Light your incense first (again, copal is traditional). See to it that you've changed out the clear glass of water on Her shrine with fresh water. Add another cookie or sweet treat as an offering, too.

How are the flowers you've offered on Tuesday faring? I like to trim the stems and change out the water in the vase on the third day of the Novena. Overall, ensure that everything is fresh and aesthetically pleasing: The Skinny Girl loves to see that the altars set up in Her honor are tidy and pretty!

As you have previously done, when you're ready to begin, make the Sign of the Cross and say the Prayer of the Most Holy Death.

INVOCATION/PRAYER OF THE MOST HOLY DEATH

Lord, before Your Divine Presence, God Almighty,
Father, Son, and Holy Spirit,
I ask for Your permission to invoke the Holy Death, *Oh Pretty Girl!*
La Niña Hermosa, I want to humbly ask that You break and destroy
All harmful spells and dark intentions of others
That may present themselves
Before my person, in my home, and on my path.
Holy Death, please relieve me of all oppression, poverty, and despair.
I ask that You please grant me _______________.
Enlighten, with Your Holy Presence, my home, my workplace,
And the environments of my loved ones.
Award us health, love, prosperity, and well-being.
Blessed and praised be Your charity, Holy Death.
Lord, I give You infinite thanks because I see Your charity.
The challenges I face every day are perfecting my spirit.
La Santísima, I give You thanks because in the midst of these challenges
I always have Your Holy Blessing.
Amen.

The main prayer of the Novena continues the energetic thread of "control and command" magic begun on day two. There's a very interesting magical correlation made (this is the essence of sympathetic magic) between a Jesus Christ Who was "defeated" on the Cross and either one's mortal enemy or the errant/non-committal romantic partner whom the petitioner desires to see equally "defeated."

If you're praying to subdue an enemy, it would be best to address this prayer to La Santa Muerte *Negra*, Patroness of Magical Defense and Offense. However, La Santa Muerte *Roja* is the Bony Lady Who oversees affairs of the heart, so if your aim is to bring back an errant lover, that petition would best be addressed to Her.

At any rate, as my *madrina* has apprised me, here's the prayer for day three of the Novena (again, having an understanding of or appreciation for the Roman Catholic cultural matrix in which these prayers were formulated is helpful):

Our Savior, Jesus Christ,
On the Cross You were defeated.
I now ask, via the intercession of The Most Holy Death,
That [NAME] will be defeated and brought low at my feet,
In the Name of the Lord!
If they are as a wild animal, they will become tame as sheep,
As pliable as the flower petals of rosemary.
Bring them to me thus.
Dear Death of my heart,
I earnestly petition you to slice open the heart of [NAME] with Your scythe.
I am all that [NAME] can see; they will desire no other but me.
Oh, *La Santísima!* Refuge and fortress!
I humbly ask that You grant me these favors that I ask of You.
To show my thanks when I see the results, I promise to light a candle
Every Monday of every week in Your honor.[‡]
Amen.

Again, follow with "The Lord's Prayer" three times.

[‡] If you promise something to La Santa Muerte, you had better keep your word!

As you did the previous day, conclude with the Closing Prayer.

CLOSING PRAYER

In Praise of the Holy Death

In the Name of the Father, and the Son, and the Holy Spirit,
Immaculate being of Light,
I implore that You grant me these favors that I ask of You.
Until the last day, hour, and second
When Your Divine Majesty *orders* me to come to Your feet,
Dear Death of My Heart,
Do not ever leave me unprotected.

DAY FOUR

The fourth day of the Novena to La Santa Muerte should occur on a Friday. If you've been paying Her proper homage all this time, you should definitely be experiencing a shift in energies surrounding the areas in your life for which you've been petitioning Her help. In my experience, She responds to prayers pretty swiftly. As with other Virgin Goddesses I venerate (such as Hel), I find that La Santa Muerte paradoxically exudes a fierce maternal protectiveness towards Her devotees.

She is so deserving of our thanks and praise! Be generous with your offerings for Her. The great Irish writer Oscar Wilde is said to have quipped, "I have very simple tastes: I simply demand the best of everything!" Let that be your guide in the quality of the heartfelt offerings you give to the Bony Lady!

As before, when you're ready to begin, make the Sign of the Cross and say the Prayer of the Most Holy Death.

INVOCATION/PRAYER OF THE MOST HOLY DEATH

Lord, before Your Divine Presence, God Almighty,
Father, Son, and Holy Spirit,
I ask for Your permission to invoke the Holy Death, *Oh Pretty Girl!*
La Niña Hermosa, I want to humbly ask that You break and destroy
All harmful spells and dark intentions of others
That may present themselves
Before my person, in my home, and on my path.
Holy Death, please relieve me of all oppression, poverty, and despair.
I ask that You please grant me _______________.
Enlighten, with Your Holy Presence, my home, my workplace,
And the environments of my loved ones.
Award us health, love, prosperity, and well-being.
Blessed and praised be Your charity, Holy Death.
Lord, I give You infinite thanks because I see Your charity.
The challenges I face every day are perfecting my spirit.
La Santísima, I give You thanks because in the midst of these challenges
I always have Your Holy Blessing.
Amen.

The main prayer of this day's Novena once again gives a tighter turn of the "control and command" magical screw that began twisting on day two. The emphasis is on not allowing your enemy to have a moment's peace until (s)he is brought low before you. Again, La Santa Muerte *Negra's* ears are the most ideal ones for such a petition.

Oh, Most Holy Death,
Empress of the Darkness,
Given the incredible Power You wield over all mortals,
I earnestly ask of You with all my heart
That [NAME] not be given shelter on this earth,
Nor a seat at any table,
Nor one moment of peace
Until they are brought to my feet, trampled under
Your foot and wholly subdued.
If [NAME] ignores Your injunction toward humility,
Then let [NAME] feel Your scythe bear down upon their head,
La Santísima!
Engulf [NAME] in Your maze of never-ending shadows, Powerful Death!
So it must be for all who come against me; they will lose.
Amen.

Again, follow with "The Lord's Prayer" three times.

As you did the previous day, conclude with the Closing Prayer.

CLOSING PRAYER

In Praise of the Holy Death

In the Name of the Father, and the Son, and the Holy Spirit,
Immaculate being of Light,
I implore that You grant me these favors that I ask of You.
Until the last day, hour, and second
When Your Divine Majesty *orders* me to come to Your feet,
Dear Death of My Heart,
Do not ever leave me unprotected.

DAY FIVE

The fifth day of the Novena to La Santa Muerte should occur on a Saturday. This day is a day of power—technically past the midpoint—in the nine-day prayer vigil and series of offerings, so you want to ensure that you're stepping up your offerings today. Show *La Santísima* that you appreciate Her for Who She is, not just what She does for you.

As before, when you're ready to begin, make the Sign of the Cross and say the Prayer of the Most Holy Death.

INVOCATION/PRAYER OF THE MOST HOLY DEATH

Lord, before Your Divine Presence, God Almighty,
Father, Son, and Holy Spirit,
I ask for Your permission to invoke the Holy Death, *Oh Pretty Girl!*
La Niña Hermosa, I want to humbly ask that You break and destroy
All harmful spells and dark intentions of others
That may present themselves
Before my person, in my home, and on my path.
Holy Death, please relieve me of all oppression, poverty, and despair.
I ask that You please grant me ______________.
Enlighten, with Your Holy Presence, my home, my workplace,
And the environments of my loved ones.
Award us health, love, prosperity, and well-being.
Blessed and praised be Your charity, Holy Death.
Lord, I give You infinite thanks because I see Your charity.
The challenges I face every day are perfecting my spirit.
La Santísima, I give You thanks because in the midst of these challenges
I always have Your Holy Blessing.
Amen.

The petition on the fifth day is to bring back a straying lover.

Glorious and Powerful Death,
My Protector and Fount of Blessings in this life,
Your force is both invincible and invisible.
I humbly ask that You turn the heart of [NAME] back to me.
May they find no pleasure or comfort in their straying path,
Nor find a partner.
May [NAME] not eat nor sleep until they are by my side.
Let their thoughts and motivation be of me and only me.
Unite our hearts in happiness and fidelity.
Amen.

Again, follow with "The Lord's Prayer" three times.

As you did the previous day, conclude with the Closing Prayer.

CLOSING PRAYER

In Praise of the Holy Death

In the Name of the Father, and the Son, and the Holy Spirit,
Immaculate being of Light,
I implore that You grant me these favors that I ask of You.
Until the last day, hour, and second
When Your Divine Majesty *orders* me to come to Your feet,
Dear Death of My Heart,
Do not ever leave me unprotected.

DAY SIX

The sixth day of the Novena to La Santa Muerte should fall on a Sunday. As it's the start of a new week, the emphasis is on purification and on cleanliness. On this day of the Novena, it's best to approach La Santa Muerte after you've had a cleansing spiritual bath, which can be as simple as adding epsom salts and either dried jasmine flowers or drops of jasmine essential oil to your hot bath water. If you're in need of healing, add hyssop as well. If you're looking to bolster your spiritual protection/psychic hygiene, rue and bergamot are good choices.

Replace any stale offerings on your shrine with fresh ones. Always change out the water in the clear chalice for La Santa Muerte on a daily basis. Light some copal incense.

As before, when you're ready to begin, make the Sign of the Cross and say the Prayer of the Most Holy Death.

INVOCATION/PRAYER OF THE MOST HOLY DEATH

Lord, before Your Divine Presence, God Almighty,
Father, Son, and Holy Spirit,
I ask for Your permission to invoke the Holy Death, *Oh Pretty Girl!*
La Niña Hermosa, I want to humbly ask that You break and destroy
All harmful spells and dark intentions of others
That may present themselves
Before my person, in my home, and on my path.
Holy Death, please relieve me of all oppression, poverty, and despair.
I ask that You please grant me ______________.
Enlighten, with Your Holy Presence, my home, my workplace,
And the environments of my loved ones.
Award us health, love, prosperity, and well-being.
Blessed and praised be Your charity, Holy Death.
Lord, I give You infinite thanks because I see Your charity.
The challenges I face every day are perfecting my spirit.
La Santísima, I give You thanks because in the midst of these challenges
I always have Your Holy Blessing.
Amen.

The petition on the sixth day is to ask for help in living a life true to one's Divinely decreed purpose. Given our fragility as mortals subject to death at any moment whenever the Holy Death ordains it, there's an understandable emotional tone of urgency.

Oh, Sovereign Lady!
Mistress of Reckonings,
Keeper of both my heart and the threads of my lifespan,
I honor You and give You thanks and praise for the numerous blessings
You bestow upon me
In the short time I walk this earth.
Sooner or later, Dear Death of my heart,
All will fall before Your scythe,
Whether old or young, rich or penniless, healthy or ill.
I earnestly beg of You that I not be taken until after I have fulfilled
My Divinely decreed mission in this life.
Teach me to walk the path of my destiny with courageous, unfaltering steps.
Should I ever stray from it, give me signs,
Oh, my Protecting Angel.
And when I am walking the road meant for me,
Give me signs to encourage taking further steps:
Let the right opportunities come to me at the right time
And through the right connections and resources.
Let my gifts be developed and shared as God wills it.
Let every step in my life's journey support my alignment with my destiny
So that when You do command me to appear before Your feet,
I will be able to leave this earth and all whom I love behind willingly,
And we will rejoice in the everlasting day.
Amen.

Again, follow with "The Lord's Prayer" three times.

As you did the previous day, conclude with the Closing Prayer.

CLOSING PRAYER

In Praise of the Holy Death

In the Name of the Father, and the Son, and the Holy Spirit,
Immaculate being of Light,
I implore that You grant me these favors that I ask of You.
Until the last day, hour, and second
When Your Divine Majesty *orders* me to come to Your feet,
Dear Death of My Heart,
Do not ever leave me unprotected.

DAY SEVEN

The seventh day of the Novena to La Santa Muerte should occur on a Monday. Today is the day to light the third of the three white, three-day glass candles that were required for the perpetual flame. Again, if at all possible, transfer, using a stick of incense or the head of a match, the flame from the second candle before it expires to the third one. As you do so, say:

"Flame to flame, the purity of my intentions is ignited."

If the second candle has already burned out, don't worry about it. Dress the third candle with any essential oils or herbs that would correspond with your intentions. Light your incense first—again, copal is traditional.

Monday is the day traditionally assigned to giving La Santa Muerte Her offerings on a weekly basis, so go all out and splurge on delectable offerings for Her shrine(s), especially as this is the last third of the Novena. Procure pretty flowers. Offer fresh water in Her clear chalice. Give Her fine chocolates. Pour some primo tequila in a shot glass. Get a decent cigar, if you're not opposed to offering tobacco, and blow some smoke in Her face before you begin your prayers.

As before, when you're ready to begin, make the Sign of the Cross and say the Prayer of the Most Holy Death.

INVOCATION/PRAYER OF THE MOST HOLY DEATH

Lord, before Your Divine Presence, God Almighty,
Father, Son, and Holy Spirit,
I ask for Your permission to invoke the Holy Death, *Oh Pretty Girl!*
La Niña Hermosa, I want to humbly ask that You break and destroy
All harmful spells and dark intentions of others
That may present themselves
Before my person, in my home, and on my path.
Holy Death, please relieve me of all oppression, poverty, and despair.
I ask that You please grant me ______________.
Enlighten, with Your Holy Presence, my home, my workplace,
And the environments of my loved ones.
Award us health, love, prosperity, and well-being.
Blessed and praised be Your charity, Holy Death.
Lord, I give You infinite thanks because I see Your charity.
The challenges I face every day are perfecting my spirit.
La Santísima, I give You thanks because in the midst of these challenges
I always have Your Holy Blessing.
Amen.

The prayer on the seventh day is short and sweet. It's a prayer for protection best addressed to *La Blanca* or *La Negra.*

Oh, Most Holy Death!
Deliver me from all evil.
Do not let me fall into any snares laid out by my enemies.
Let their negative intentions redound on their own heads a thousand-fold
As I go about my life unscathed! *Ashé!*
You have my love and my steadfast loyalty,
My Protector and Mistress.
I humbly ask that You concede all the favors that I ask of You
In this Novena.
Amen.

Again, follow with "The Lord's Prayer" three times.

As you did the previous day, conclude with the Closing Prayer.

CLOSING PRAYER

In Praise of the Holy Death

In the Name of the Father, and the Son, and the Holy Spirit,
Immaculate being of Light,
I implore that You grant me these favors that I ask of You.
Until the last day, hour, and second
When Your Divine Majesty *orders* me to come to Your feet,
Dear Death of My Heart,
Do not ever leave me unprotected.

DAY EIGHT

The eighth day of the Novena to La Santa Muerte should take place on a Tuesday. Check to see how the three-day candle you lit yesterday is faring. Is the flame burning steadily and cleanly? Is the glass clear? Or has a dark layer of soot, representing an obstacle to the fulfillment of your prayers, formed at the lip of the glass? Overall, what sort of vibration does your shrine to *La Santísima* exude? How content does She seem to be with your offerings?

As before, when you're ready to begin, make the Sign of the Cross and say the Prayer of the Most Holy Death.

INVOCATION/PRAYER OF THE MOST HOLY DEATH

Lord, before Your Divine Presence, God Almighty,
Father, Son, and Holy Spirit,
I ask for Your permission to invoke the Holy Death, *Oh Pretty Girl!*
La Niña Hermosa, I want to humbly ask that You break and destroy
All harmful spells and dark intentions of others
That may present themselves
Before my person, in my home, and on my path.
Holy Death, please relieve me of all oppression, poverty, and despair.
I ask that You please grant me _______________.
Enlighten, with Your Holy Presence, my home, my workplace,
And the environments of my loved ones.
Award us health, love, prosperity, and well-being.
Blessed and praised be Your charity, Holy Death.
Lord, I give You infinite thanks because I see Your charity.
The challenges I face every day are perfecting my spirit.
La Santísima, I give You thanks because in the midst of these challenges
I always have Your Holy Blessing.
Amen.

The petition on the eighth day returns us to the controlling form of love magic that we first encountered on day two. The petitioner seeking to have an errant lover return to them would be best advised to pray to La Santa Muerte *Roja*, She Who hears the prayers of the lovelorn, the betrayed, the lustful, the happily coupled, and the broken-hearted.

In addition to the white three-day glass candle burning for this last leg of the Novena, you may want to adorn your shrine with a red glass candle bearing La Santa Muerte *Roja's* image. Fix or dress that candle's wax with "Adam & Eve" oil (even if this is for a same-sex partnership: the metaphor of attraction is what's being worked here regardless of the pairing of genitalia involved), "Come to Me" incense powder (available at any *botanica*), rose oil, and powdered jasmine flower petals or jasmine essential oil. A drop of "Dragon's Blood" oil to expedite the working of the spell may be added at the end.

Let us pray:

Oh, La Santa Muerte! Holy Death of Majesty!
Given Your immense power over all mortal desire,
I ask that You bring me back the companionship, the affection,
And the loyalty of [NAME].
Do not give them one moment's peace
Should they be with someone else.
Do not even allow the company of friends and family without me
To bring them happiness.
Let [NAME] know that I summon them forth,
Bring their straying feet back to my doorstep.
No peace will be given unto [NAME] otherwise.
When they sleep, let them dream of me.
When awake, make them think of me lovingly and loyally.
These words I declare to You, Most Holy Death.
Enforce my summons.
Let [NAME] feel Your power.
Grant me what I ask; fulfill this Novena.
Amen.

Again, follow with "The Lord's Prayer" three times.

As you did the previous day, conclude with the Closing Prayer.

CLOSING PRAYER

In Praise of the Holy Death

In the Name of the Father, and the Son, and the Holy Spirit,
Immaculate being of Light,
I implore that You grant me these favors that I ask of You.
Until the last day, hour, and second
When Your Divine Majesty *orders* me to come to Your feet,
Dear Death of My Heart,
Do not ever leave me unprotected.

DAY NINE

The ninth and final day of the Novena to La Santa Muerte should occur on a Wednesday. The third of the three-day white glass candles burned in Her honor should be close to burning itself out.

Take time for quiet contemplation of the entire Novena experience: How did your devotional relationship with *La Santísima* deepen? In what ways have you changed, perhaps your attitude towards your own mortality? Or your understanding of the nature of prayer in general, or its contextualization in Mexican folk religion in particular?

Have any portents presented themselves at any time during the Novena, assuring you that *La Flaquíta* has, in fact, been listening to you? Did you feel Her bony fingers steering your ship of destiny in the past nine days in any way? Journal about your experiences.

Synchronicities often abound. And it has always been my experience that my prayers manifested pretty quickly, especially if I was seeking payback against an enemy.

She is a Lady of Miracles, and thanks and praise are due to Her always. Hence, for the final day of the Novena, be sure to go all out with your devotional offerings: not just flowers, but a bouquet of roses, Godiva chocolates, primo tequila, and choice tobacco or even a blunt of Mary Jane. You get the idea.

As before, when you're ready to begin, make the Sign of the Cross and say the Prayer of the Most Holy Death.

INVOCATION/PRAYER OF THE MOST HOLY DEATH

Lord, before Your Divine Presence, God Almighty,
Father, Son, and Holy Spirit,
I ask for Your permission to invoke the Holy Death, *Oh Pretty Girl!*
La Niña Hermosa, I want to humbly ask that You break and destroy
All harmful spells and dark intentions of others
That may present themselves
Before my person, in my home, and on my path.
Holy Death, please relieve me of all oppression, poverty, and despair.
I ask that You please grant me _______________.
Enlighten, with Your Holy Presence, my home, my workplace,
And the environments of my loved ones.
Award us health, love, prosperity, and well-being.
Blessed and praised be Your charity, Holy Death.
Lord, I give You infinite thanks because I see Your charity.
The challenges I face every day are perfecting my spirit.
La Santísima, I give You thanks because in the midst of these challenges
I always have Your Holy Blessing.
Amen.

Let us pray:

Oh, Holy Death!
My ever-vigilant Protector!
Great Liberator!
By all the virtues granted unto You by God,
I ask that You liberate me from all forms of sickness, from pain,
From despair, from poverty, and from the snares of my foes.
Do not let anyone who bears me ill will,
Do not let any wagging tongue speaking out against me,
Form negativity that coalesces and rises up against me.
Instead, let such evil intentions redound on the heads of the senders
A thousand times over, *Ashé!*
As I go about my life unscathed.
You Who are the Right Hand of God,
Award me opportunities that promote my expansion and development,
Ones that align me with my destiny.
Grant me luck, health, meaningful work, and abundance in all of its forms.
Open my roads favorably
And allow only true friends to serve as companions on the journey;
Shut the doors against all who mean me harm.
Cut out with Your scythe from my path all smiling enemies, all false friends.

May I live a long and joyous life, rich with purpose,
One that will have me glorifying You always.
For You reign in my heart,
O Empress of This World,
And I pray that each day I will be a more fitting vessel of
Your Grace and Mercy,
That I may share it with all.
Amen.

Again, follow with "The Lord's Prayer" three times.

As you did the previous day, conclude with the Closing Prayer.

CLOSING PRAYER

In Praise of the Holy Death

In the Name of the Father, and the Son, and the Holy Spirit,
Immaculate being of Light,
I implore that You grant me these favors that I ask of You.
Until the last day, hour, and second
When Your Divine Majesty *orders* me to come to Your feet,
Dear Death of My Heart,
Do not ever leave me unprotected.

Afterword

Obviously, the *cultus* of the Bony Lady is not for everyone. For conservative North American Christians (Catholics and Protestants both) and quartz crystal-clutching New Agers alike, La Santa Muerte's images and cultic practices conjure revulsion at best and accusations of diabolism at worst. She suffers from the same bad PR as "naughty" Divinities like Set, Loki, and the *Exu* of Brazilian *Quimbanda*.

But for the hardy souls She chooses to claim as Her own, there exists when praying to Her, if I may be so bold as to borrow words from the Bible, "the peace which passeth all understanding" (Philippians 4:6).

Mysteries are experience-based; they can't be presented and assessed through the bifurcated, limited medium of human language. Speaking for myself and for the other *Muertistas* I know, the number-one motivational force in praying to La Santa Muerte is a deep and abiding love for Her. *For Who She is.* Not for what She does or is capable of doing on your behalf.

That being said, She is a Being of Darkness. If you're not already comfortable with darkness and the myriad forms it takes in the human experience, chances are slim indeed that you'd find yourself called to serve La Santa Muerte.

And darkness...*seeps.* Its nature is to expand. A conscious commitment to it alters your perceptions, makes you feel at home in its inky domain.

Prepare to have your psychic doors blown open, prepare to have experiences with the spirits of the dead as you maintain your steadfast devotion to *La Santísima.* (Or perhaps, your current state of openness/psychic development and/or communion with the dead already marks you as Hers.) Some folks won't like this, but it's a natural by-product of loving Her and electing to be in Her service. Nietzsche's famous quip about having the darkness stare back into you the longer you stare into it is one-hundred percent applicable here.

In the course of when I first performed this Novena while writing about it daily on my blog for nine nights in November of 2015, I distinctly recall, and my journal reminds me, that I had evidence of my prayers being answered as early as the morning of day two: A longstanding rival/enemy of mine at work in my cut-throat industry of advertising announced his resignation, a complete and total surprise to all, myself included. I also recall just acutely feeling La Santa Muerte's Presence throughout my home (a Chicago condo built, incidentally, atop a mass paupers' graveyard!), but especially in the primary bedroom, where I kept my shrines to Her.

For these occurrences and the others that I haven't named, I give thanks. I give thanks for the Presence, Power, and Majesty of the Most Holy Death. I give constant thanks for Her ongoing protection of my personhood and those of my loved ones, spiritually and physically.

I give thanks for the joy that serving Her brings. I give thanks for the ease of acceptance of my own mortality that praying to Her brings.

Whatever your spiritual tradition, give your Powers thanks on a regular basis. The more you express your gratitude vocally, the more you will be given opportunities to express thanks for even greater blessings. May you think and act on an attitude of gratitude mindfully each and every day, whichever Goddesses and Gods you serve.

So mote it be!

Appendices

APPENDIX A:

"VIRGIN DEATH GODDESSES: HEL, LA SANTA MUERTE, AND YEWA": TRANSCRIPT OF A LECTURE GIVEN AT THE 24th ANNUAL FELLOWSHIP OF ISIS CHICAGO GODDESS CONVENTION, SATURDAY, OCTOBER 18, 2017

It's always a pleasure to be speaking here and meeting so many wonderful new folks. Thank you all for coming. Quick show of hands: who here honors a Death God or Goddess in their personal devotional practices?

I'm a Polytheist devoted to such Goddesses, and I'd like to spend some time with you discussing three in particular: the Norse Goddess Hel; Mexico's La Santa Muerte, a.k.a. The Holy Death; and the Nigerian Orisha, Yewa—Who They are, Why They matter, and how you can cultivate a devotional relationship with Them if you so choose.

What's striking about these Death Deities of various cultures—northern European, North American, and West African, respectively—that I'm going to talk about is that they're gendered female and they're regarded as "virgins," so we have a lot of intersectionality to examine when we focus on what we know about each Goddess historically and what we know about Them in contemporary worship.

But before we start discussing each of these three Goddesses, I've got a couple thoughts on what significance the issue of gender bears as well as the virginity angle when we're looking at Death Goddesses.

Gender and Virginity

If you think about why there are female Death Deities to begin with—especially in such disparate cultures as medieval Scandinavia and modern Nigeria—the answer may lie in the fact that throughout the world, dealing with death is women's work. Women tend to the dying and women prepare the dead for burial or cremation: they wash the corpses; they sit in vigil; and they perform elaborate mourning rites publicly and privately. In the archetypal, cross-cultural image of the Earth Mother Who gives us all life, She also takes life back into Her; the womb becomes the yawning grave. So female Death Deities very much make sense to us.

But why are these Goddesses "virgin" ones?

In our current discourse in the Western world, the word "virgin" is usually a strict, almost clinically defined term characterizing a person who has not had sexual intercourse (for women, the hymen has remained intact). In pop culture, such individuals are invariably made fun of—they're socially awkward for missing out on sex; they're seen as pitiable, their lack of experience to be remedied immediately. They're seen, in other words, as fundamentally *disempowered* individuals.

But there is another side to this coin, and we have to turn to the remote past in Western culture, where the word "virgin" was itself was a gendered word—gendered as female—and it connoted empowerment. Why? In classical Greece, as feminist scholar Barbara Walker informs us, the word "virgin" meant "a woman who was whole unto herself" (1048-1049). In other words, she was an unmarried woman, meaning her identity—her station in the world—was not defined through her relationship to a man.

It was not a comment on lack of participation in sexual activity. We've all heard of the famous Vestal Virgins of ancient Rome; their cult was tremendously important to the spiritual health and well-being of the Roman state. They belonged to no man, but to all of Rome, and there are records of them as having been quite sexually active—with each other and with the chief state priest known as the *pontifex maximus,* who orchestrated public rituals done on behalf of the state (Walker 1046). As an aside, the Catholic Church stole, among other thefts from Paganism in antiquity, the title of *pontifex maximus* (the "ultimate bridge"—i.e., between mortals and the Gods) and applied it to the Pope!

So these Virgin Goddesses are Whole unto Themselves; thus, unlike other Goddesses you may revere, these Fierce Ladies are not defined in relationship to a male consort/partner/twin, and They are therefore powerful solo acts. To quote the Eurythmics song from the mid-80s, "Sisters Are Doin' It For Themselves!"

There is an added element of purity to these Goddesses as well—meaning that They are free from spiritual pollution and they offer that purity to Their devotees. Some may demand a rigorous level of purity from Their followers; this is especially true in the case of Yewa, as we'll see.

So let's take a closer look at the histories and the living cults of the three Virgin Death Goddesses that are my focus today: Hel, La Santa Muerte, and Yewa.

Hel

The Teutonic peoples of continental Europe and Scandinavia all knew Hel, and Her lore was widely popularized in the Viking era thanks to the thirteenth-century writings of an Icelander named Snorri Sturluson, a learned statesman and poet who, although Christian, sought to preserve the older, oral literature tradition describing the great deeds of the Old Norse Gods, the tribes of the Aesir and the Vanir. He compiled these bardic tales in the *Poetic Edda* and the *Prose Edda* so that he could teach future generations of Icelandic poets the proper way to relate these tales. And it's from these texts that we learn about Hel and Her family.

The Goddess Hel—sometimes called "Hela," spelled with one "l" or two— is a Giant, one of the *Jötunn*. Her father is the so-called Trickster God, Loki, and Her mother, the fierce Angrboda, the wolf-witch of the Iron Wood.

Hel has two brothers: the world-encircling serpent, Jörmungandr; and the wolf, Fenrir. The God Odin, Whose sight surveys all of the Nine Worlds in the Norse Cosmos, was so upset by the prophecies concerning these Wyrd children of Loki's—and the role each would have in disturbing events to come, including the end of the world—that He sought to avert Fate by mitigating each child's Power.

Here's how Snurri Sturluson relates it in the *Prose Edda:*

> When they came to him he threw the serpent into the deep sea, which surrounds all lands. There waxed the serpent so that he lies in the midst of the ocean, surrounds all the earth, and bites his own tail. Hel he cast into Niflheim, and gave her power over nine worlds, that she should appoint abodes to them that are sent to her, namely, those who die from sickness or old age. She has there a great mansion, and the walls around it are of strange height, and the gates are huge. (Chapter IX, para. 2, lines 4-7)

Odin was most creeped out by Hel and had such an aversion to Her that He banished Her into the world farthest away from His own, a section of Niflheim—the Land Below of Mist and Cold; it is located under the roots of the World Tree—that She could rule over, and called it Helheim. To Hel would go all those who die of sickness and old age— deaths not heroic enough to merit Odin's company in the hereafter. Odin declared that Hela would never, ever be allowed to set foot in Asgard, the most "heavenly" of the Nine Worlds, and so, according to the lore, She never has.

What's striking about Hel, as Snorri describes Her appearance, is how She's divided into a living half and a dead half.

> One-half of her is blue, and the other half is of the hue of flesh; hence she is easily known. Her looks are very stern and grim.
> (*Prose Edda,* Chapter IX, para. 2, lines 8-9)

Northern Tradition Polytheist and spirit worker Raven Kaldera likens Hel's presence to that of a black hole (*Jotunbok* 292). But She gives peace and rest and Her home of Helheim can be accessed—up to a point—in shamanic journeys and visions (291).

According to Heathen *gythia* and founder of The Troth, Diana Paxson, "Hella guards the ancestors whose folkways we are trying to restore" (*Essential Ásatrú* 94).

Thus, having Hel in a place of prominence at your ancestor shrine is ideal. I find Her energies to be very kind to the dead and hospitable, as though She were a shepherd of the dead. It's customary for me to do a Hel-blot on a Saturday; that's the day of the week I also honor Her father, Loki.

I also find Hel extremely encouraging in the act of contemplating your own mortality as well as in honoring the cycle of decay—something our death-sanitizing culture is wildly uncomfortable with. "That's the core of Hela's mystery," writes Raven Kaldera. "The things about her appearance that are the most grotesque are the holiest" (*Jotunbok* 301).

Offerings to Hela typically include dark and bitter foods and kinds of alcohol, from rye bread, to hearty stews to stout, or dry red wines. Mead, of course, is traditional. Blood is an appropriate offering: your own or that of an animal that would have been recognized as a food source in Northern Europe. She also appreciates dried, well-preserved flowers—especially dried roses (Kaldera 294). Northern Tradition priest and spirit worker Galina Krasskova also suggests dark chocolate and even coffee beans (*Northern Tradition* 234). Any food offerings left on Her shrine have to remain until they're good and rotten.

Let's chant this chant to Hel:

> "Lady of the Darkness,
> Ruler of the night,
> We sleep within thy shadows
> To wake into thy light."
> (Paxson, *Essential Ásatrú,* 95)

La Santa Muerte

And so we travel from the cold land of Hel to the warmth and the vibrancy of Mexico's fastest-growing "folk saint" La Santa Muerte, "The Holy Death." Here we have the striking image of the skeleton, androgynous on its own, now gendered as female and seen as immensely powerful—one of Her epithets, in fact, is *La Dama Poderosa*, "The Powerful Lady."

But she inspires such affectionate devotion and is given cutesy epithets like *La Niña Bonita*, the "Pretty Girl," and *La Flaquita*, "Skinny Girl." She is Mexico's "Skeleton Saint," and Her fame and cult following have been steadily expanding north of the border for decades now (Chestnut 10).

Glass candles in a variety of wax colors (the color correspondences are important, as you'll find out) bearing Her image and featuring bilingual prayers in Spanish and English can now routinely be found in virtually every grocery store's Latino foods section, shelved next to candles depicting familiar Roman Catholic saints venerated in the Americas like La Virgen de Guadalupe and San Miguel (Chestnut 9).

La Santa Muerte's popularity is meeting with fierce resistance (Chestnut 12, 189). In fact, the Roman Catholic Church and evangelical Protestant churches are actively campaigning/propagandizing in Mexico—with the full blessing of the right-wing Mexican government—to denounce the cult of La Santa Muerte as, you guessed it, "Satanic," sensationalizing Her worship in true yellow journalism tradition and tarnishing Her legions of devotees as murderous drug traffickers engaged in immoral, downright criminal rituals that are horrible enough to even include human sacrifice (Chestnut 10).

Why the hateful lies? Because La Santísima offers Freedom. Freedom is unquestionably La Santa Muerte's greatest blessing to Her devotees. Freedom from judgment. Freedom from self-imposed limitations. Freedom from the fear of death.

Running a close second is Her ability to grant protection on the physical and astral planes: the reason why both criminals *and* members of law enforcement/the military in Mexico invoke Her for aid in their daily work (Chestnut 19, 108).

The third reason why people are drawn to Her cult is that people who consider themselves to be good Catholics naturally first tried praying to the Christian "God the Father" of their catechism or to various saints for help in their dire situations, only to have those prayers unanswered. Dejected and desperate, they subsequently turned their attention to the welcoming grin of *La Santísima*, and then they experienced profound epiphanies when it was clear She answered their prayers (Prower 15).

She is known, incidentally, for quick turn-around time in answering prayers (Chestnut 59, 192).

She has found many champions from the ranks of the working poor as well as sex workers, Queer folks, trans folks, unwed mothers, the incarcerated—people whose lifestyles fall outside the pale of the Church's compassion (Rollin 20).

La Santa Muerte has various aspects based on color correspondences, but the three most popular are also, interestingly, the colors of the Goddess as those who are familiar with Paganism will recognize: red, black, and white. *La Santa Muerte Roja* is Whom we turn to for the affairs of the heart. *La Santa Muerte Negra* is prayed to for protection and concealment, as well as hexing and acts of vengeance. *La Santa Muerta Blanca* affords magical defense and the safeguarding of purity—this is the Virgin in our modern sense of "purity" and being "untainted" by sexual energies.

Offerings to La Santa Muerte include candy, expensive chocolates, fresh flowers, fruit, grain (She's a Reaper) or whole wheat bread, or white bread rolls you can get in a Mexican bakery called *bolillo* (Chestnut 78). She's fond of liquor but it's essential that She be given a glass of water on Her shrine, one that is refreshed every day. It's said that She craves water to slake Her immense thirst from all the traveling She does around the world to answer folks' prayers (Chestnut 72).

In terms of book recommendations to learn more about Her, there's no better English-language book on the market than Dr. Andrew Chestnut's *Devoted to Death*. He is an anthropologist who has been studying La Santa Muerte's rapidly growing cult in Mexico for the past 30 years. He is also a devotee.

If you're a native Spanish speaker, lucky you, you've got a lot of books published in Mexico that provide details on ritual practices for the different aspects or "colors" of *La Santísima*, not the least of which is an actual *Biblia de La Santa Muerte*.

I don't have that book but I do have a Spanish-language La Santa Muerte Tarot deck.[§] My best friend moved back to his native Texas a few years ago and he bought this for me at a *botanica* in San Antonio. I absolutely *love* the artwork. Come see me afterwards if you want to take a look at it.

---

§ If you're curious, it's the *Tarot de la Santa Muerte*, © 2014 Berbera Editores. Illustrated by Roberto Castro. It features several versions of The World card showcasing La Santa Muerte in Her different robes; I adore it and I often display the cards on my various shrines to *La Santísima*.

Yewa

So, moving right along: the Virgin Death Goddess Who has gotten the least amount of press that I'm aware of is the Orisha Yewa, the Maiden of the Cemetery.

Her cult originated in the Yoruban religion of Ifá in Nigeria and has proliferated in the New World African diaspora religious offshoots of Candomblé and Santería (González-Wippler 252).

Yewa is regarded as a literal virgin, a maiden. Because of the fact that Her personality is said to be severe and harsh (González-Wippler 65), there are strict protocols on how to invoke and placate Her. It generally is something seen as an initiates-only level of experience—Ifá and Santería, if you didn't know, are initiatory religions—and one has to abide by a world of taboos.

Some versions of the sacred stories told in Ifá and Santería relate that all of the Orisha were once human beings Who became Deified because of extraordinary acts that They performed while alive (González-Wippler 40).

In the case of Yewa, there's an inversion because the lore is that She died an untimely death; therefore, She didn't reach Goddesshood because She performed an extraordinary feat. Fittingly, She thus rules over the class of spirits known as *abiku* in Nigerian lore—*abiku* literally means "predestined to death"—these are restless spirits of dead children, restless because their life force potential remains unfulfilled (Neimark 47).

It would take an Orisha of great purity to serve as the leader of these spirits, so perhaps that's why there's such an emphasis on strict ritual protocol and the observance of taboos, such as not invoking Her when you're having your period or if you're pregnant or plan on becoming pregnant.

Unlike the other Death Goddesses we've discussed, Who bear skeletal or partially skeletal faces, Yewa has Her face covered, it is said, out of modesty due to Her virginal purity. But it is also implied that Her Mysteries are concealed, and, again, those Mysteries are not for the uninitiated. Hence the veil.

In Santería, She is syncretized with St. Clare of Assisi, a saint who died young—obviously, a virgin—and was known for her humility, her piety, and her charity towards all living things, just like her good friend St. Francis of Assisi (González-Wippler 65). St. Clare founded the Order of the Poor Clares. If you're curious, St. Clare's Feast Day is August 11.

Unlike St. Clare, Yewa is said to be unforgiving (González-Wippler 65). If you offend Her by botching up ritual protocol, for example, She just might react in a vindictive manner. She cannot be "bribed" with offerings the way that some other Orisha might.

And when it comes to offerings, a lot of Her offerings overlap with that of the Orisha Oyá. Oyá is the Warrior Orisha Who rules hurricanes, the winds of change, the marketplace, and the gates of the cemetery; She is not a Death Deity, however (Neimark 128). Yewa rules inside the cemetery, so that's the best place to leave offerings for Her. Offerings, as with Oyá, are typically nine in number.

Like a lot of preteen or adolescent girls the world over, Yewa loves the color pink—so pink flowers such as roses would be ideal to offer Her (González-Wippler 65). She also takes dark foods like plums, red pears, black grapes, eggplant—either nine eggplants or nine slices of a really large eggplant—red wine or dark rum (poured into the ground), pieces of roast pork (pigs are a chthonic animal, offered to death and underworld Deities across the world), heaping piles of black beans or black-eyed peas, dark chocolate, and black hens are also sacrificed to her.

It is said that Yewa loves to dance on graves—Her movements are very sharp and staccato—and She whips Her sacred implement of power, a fly whisk known as an *irukere*, around (González-Wippler 262). When Her devotees get possessed at a *bembé*, a ritual to honor the Orisha or the dead that features live drumming, they twirl about in their many-layered skirts and whip the floor and other people with their fly whisks.

I'm going to play a little bit of a recording of a devotional song that is played in Her honor in Ifá. As you listen to it, what does it evoke for you? How does it help you discern Yewa's energies?

Conclusion

Well, I thank you for joining me on this global tour of three Virgin Death Goddesses Whom I serve. I hope that you've enjoyed it and that if you have any questions, please come up and see me. I also invite everyone to come up to the communal ancestor altar and contribute an image of a Death Deity they honor or a photo of a deceased loved one.

Thank you, and I hope you all have a wonderful time at this 24th annual Fellowship of Isis in Chicago Goddess Convention!

APPENDIX B:

SPIRITUAL CLEANSING IN IFÁ: "SOUR" AND "SWEET" BATHS

Many religions advocate the removal of spiritual pollution (what the ancient Greeks called *miasma*) through a variety of methods; in Ifá, as in related African Diaspora Religions (ADRs) like Vodoun and Santería, ritual baths comprised of sacred herbs and other organic ingredients are commonly prescribed for the removal of negative energy from one's head (the locus of personal destiny) and home environment.

While some baths are for initiates only, meaning they are comprised of blessed ingredients arduously prepared—under the benevolent auspices of the *Orisha* Òsanyìn, Lord of the Forest and Master of Plants and Herbal Medicine—over a span of days by one's godparents and other trained clergy in the religion, the ones the Orisha prescribed for me in a recent Ifá reading are ones I was meant to prepare myself. They are baths anyone could easily do, whether they adhere to any of the ADRs or not. Since they're easily adaptable to any religious tradition and made of readily available ingredients (i.e., they're probably already in your kitchen pantry), I thought I'd share with you how you go about preparing for the series of ritual cleansings known as "sour" and "sweet" baths.

First Sour, Then Sweet

There are a total of three baths: one "sour," two "sweet." They are meant to be taken every other day, so if you start your sour bath on a Saturday, for example, then the first sweet bath would take place on Monday and the second sweet bath on a Wednesday.

The time of day is important, as are other ritual gestures, which I'll describe in a moment: the sour bath ideally starts just after sunset, as the forces of darkness gain strength. The two sweet baths, by contrast, should be taken at sunrise, honoring the powers of light and new beginnings.

The purpose of the sour bath is to acknowledge that your life experiences are currently bitter ones, for a variety of reasons: illness, losses, grief, financial hardship, relationship problems, legal issues, psychic attack, or even just a feeling of "stuckness."

Your energy levels are low; you feel depleted and defeated. The emphasis, aptly enough, is on having bitter herbs included in your bath. As you immerse yourself in the waters of the sour bath, you pay the forces of negativity culpable for your distress their due. You recognize that they've brought you to this state, but the tide will imminently turn in your favor.

This is what you'll need for the sour bath:

- A pair of tea light candles, which will be lit and positioned on the sides of the tub

- Flowers with red or purple petals (I used the entire heads of red chrysanthemums)

- Fresh, dried, or powdered bitter herbs, such as stinging nettle, dandelion, horehound, wormwood, yarrow

- A half cup of vinegar (whether white, red, or apple cider makes no difference)

- Seven drops of ammonia (seven being the number of evil in Ifá)

- An empty cup

Procedure: Conventionally clean out your bathtub beforehand. As sunset commences, fill up the tub with hot water, as hot as you can stand it. Light the tea light candles and turn off all electric lights in your vicinity.

Toss in all of the ingredients cited above. If you don't want to run the risk of clogging up your drain with the herbs and flower petals, it's okay to have them tied in separate tea bags or one large organza bag and then immersed in the hot water.

When you're ready to enter the tub, do so through the "gateway" of the two lit candles placed on opposing sides of your tub. You will exit by standing up and stepping out from between those candles also.

As you're in the tub, inhaling the scent of the bitter herbs and the ammonia and vinegar, think of the difficulties you're experiencing in your life and how badly you want them to change. As you sit and meditate and/or pray to your Powers to help you, make sure that you dunk yourself below the water's surface—completely covering your head—for a total of seven times in the course of your bath.

You basically want to stay in it until the water begins to cool off. When it does so and you're ready to exit, again, step out of the tub through the "gateway" of the lit candles as when you entered. As the water drains, reach for your empty cup and scoop up some of the bath water to the rim of the cup—this is for an important follow-up step once you're dry.

I have to stress that *you are not supposed to towel dry* after taking *any* kind of spiritual bath in Ifá—let your hair and skin air dry.

It's time-consuming, yes, and for us ladies the effect is sure to be one of a bad hair day, but the plant medicine is supposed to be given the chance to literally get soaked up by your body so you can internalize the effects.

Once you're dry, put on your bathrobe or some dark-colored clothes and grab that cup of sour bath water with some of the ingredients that were floating around in it. You're going to go outdoors and face west.

Holding your cup over your head, say words to the following effect (substituting your Deity or Deities of choice if the Yoruban tradition isn't what you practice):

> *"Ifá, My Father in Heaven Who knows and sees all, I have given the Ajogun** Their due. I declare Their hold on me broken! As I cast this water into the west, so, too, do I cast out of my head and my life all of my problems. Ashé, ashé, ashé!"* ††

Go back indoors and if you live with another person or people, announce that you need some alone time. Be sure to drink lots of room-temperature water to replenish your body; you've sweated out a lot of toxins in the course of that hot bath.

Do calming things that promote self-care as the evening wears on and you prepare for bed: avoid the TV/news, take time to write in a journal, do some stretches, give thanks to the Power or Powers you serve at your altar. Hopefully, you will feel supremely relaxed and ready to transition into a night of restful sleep.

How Sweet It Is!

Whereas the first of the three baths, the sour bath, is intended to take place at sunset, the two baths that round out this series of spiritual cleansings are sweet baths intended to take place at sunrise. Remember, you're spacing the baths every other day.

When it's the morning of your first sweet bath, gather together the following:

- A pair of tea light candles, which will be lit and positioned on the sides of the tub

- Flowers with all-white petals (the heads of daisies, lilies, roses, or white chrysanthemums are all good choices)

- Fresh, dried, or powdered healing herbs, five in number: I used allspice, angelica, comfrey, hyssop, and rue

- A small bottle or jar of honey (the teddy bear-shaped ones are ideal)

- Three cups of milk

- Powdered cinnamon and nutmeg and whole nutmegs, if available

- One raw egg, having the yolk is critical

** Collective name for the forces of darkness in Ifá; literally witches said to sit at the left hand of the Creator.
†† *Ashé* is Yoruban for "May it be so!"

- Drops of your favorite perfume or cologne
- An empty cup
- *Optional:* Holy Water
- *Optional:* cocoa butter or shea butter

Procedure: Again, if you don't want to risk clogging your drain, enclose the flower petals, herbs, and whole nutmeg in separate tea bags or a large organza or cotton bag to steep them in.

Make sure your tub is spotlessly clean before you begin running the hot water to fill the tub—as before, make it as hot as you can withstand.

Light the tea light candles and turn off all electric lights in your vicinity.

Crack the egg first and toss it in before any of the other ingredients— my water was so hot the egg actually cooked! Throw in the flowers and herbs, the powdered cinnamon and nutmeg (they will make the tub smell so *gooooood!*), and then the milk and honey. Save your favorite perfume or cologne as a finishing touch.

As before, enter the tub through the "gateway" of the lit candles.

This is the joyous part. As you sit in the hot water, smelling the sweet ingredients, think of the ways that all the sweet things in life are already on their way to you, thanks to the grace of the Divine and your own destiny. Be open towards receiving these blessings.

Immerse yourself underwater a total of five times—five being the number of the *Orisha* Oshun, a powerful *Orisha* of rivers. (There is a river in Nigeria's Osogbo state named after Her; Her sacred grove on its banks is a UNESCO World Heritage Site.) Oshun's *ashé* ensures that into our lives flow abundance in all of its forms: money, beauty, pleasure, and lap-it-up, honey-sweet sexual healing—the good things of life, indeed!

When the water has sufficiently cooled, it's time to exit the tub by stepping out between the lit candles. Once again, as the water drains, take your empty cup and scoop up some of the bath water with the array of ingredients, especially the flower petals and whole nutmeg.

Let yourself air dry as before. Once you're dry, put on white or light-colored clothes; Oshun is fond of gold and orange, but light green is also a good choice (the combination of green and gold happen to be the *Orisha* Ifá's signature colors).

Take your cup of bath water and go outdoors, but this time you're going to face east.

As you behold the beauty of a new day dawning and its promise of possibilities, hold your cup aloft and say words such as:

> *"Ifá, My Father in Heaven Who knows and sees all, I welcome with open arms all of the sweet things in life that are on their way to me now! As I cast this water into the east, may it serve as an invitation for my own Orí and Mother Oshun to bless me with health, prosperity, love, and happiness! Ashé, ashé, ashé!"*

Toss out the water and blissfully welcome those blessings you've invoked!

This process is to be repeated two mornings hence—remember, you're taking two sweet baths to make the total of cleansing baths three in number (one sour, two sweet). I guarantee you that on the morning of your third and final bath, you'll be feeling uplifted, energized, hopeful, and excited about receiving the blessings that are on their way to you! It's definitely worth the trade-off of having a bad hair day! But hey, egg is good protein for your hair follicles.

I really do encourage you to give these spiritual baths a try the next time you're having a case of "the ick."

May the *Orisha* and your own *Orí*—the Destiny you signed up for before the Throne of the Creator when you consented to incarnate— always help you walk the path of power through purity! *Ashé!*

Works Cited and Suggested Reading

Chestnut, R. Andrew. *Devoted to Death: Santa Muerte, The Skeleton Saint.* Oxford: Oxford University Press, 2012.

DiGregorio, Sophia. *Grimoire of Santa Muerte (2-vol.).* Lexington, KY: Winter Tempest Books, 2013.

Dorsey, Lilith. *Orishas, Goddesses, and Voodoo Queens: The Divine Feminine in the African Religious Traditions.* Newburyport, MA: Weiser Books, 2020.

Gonzalez-Wippler, Migene. *Santería: The Religion.* St. Paul, MN: Llewellyn Publications, 1989.

Kaldera, Raven. *The Jotunbok: Working with the Giants of the Northern Tradition. Northern Tradition Shamanism, Book I.* Hubbardston, MA: Asphodel Press, 2006.

Krasskova, Galina and Raven Kaldera. *Northern Tradition for the Solitary Practitioner.* Franklin Lakes, NJ: New Page Books, 2009.

Neimark, Philip John Neimark. *The Way of the Orisa.* New York: HarperCollins, 1993.

Paxson, Diana. *Essential Ásatrú: Walking the Path of Norse Paganism.* New York: Citadel Press, 2006.

Prower, Tomás. *La Santa Muerte: Unearthing the Magic & Mysticism of Death.* Woodbury, MN: Llewellyn Worldwide, 2015.

Rollin, Tracey. *Santa Muerte: The History, Rituals, and Magic of Our Lady of the Holy Death.* Newburyport, MA: Weiser Books, 2017.

Sturluson, Snorri. *The Prose Edda: Norse Mythology.* Available at: http://www.gutenberg.org/files/18947/18947-h/18947-h.htm.

Walker, Barbara. *The Woman's Encyclopedia of Myths and Secrets.* New York: HarperCollins, 1983.

About the Author

Rev. Anna Applegate (*née* Urosevich) is a Chicago native and first-generation Serbian American who was taught to believe in the Spirit World and the beneficent intervention of her ancestors in daily life from a very early age. A Queer Witch and pious Polytheist who tends to roll out a welcome mat to chthonic Deities in particular, she became active in the Chicago Fellowship of Isis (FOI) community in 2002 and received her legal ordination as a Priestess sworn to serve the Goddesses Nebet-Het (Nephthys), Bast, and Hekate Khthonia by the Lady Loreon Vigné at The Temple of Isis, Geyserville, California, in 2012. The following year, Anna's shrines grew by One more as she welcomed La Santa Muerte into her private and public ritual workings.

Anna is the founder of the FOI-chartered Iseum of the Rekhet Akhu, whose mission is to highlight the interrelatedness of the communities of the living and the dead and to cultivate transfigured spirits (*Akhu*) in human form through the Egyptian tradition of temple ritual magic. Anna is also an initiate in the West African Traditional Religion of Ifá; her godfather's House is based in Chicago. As if this plethora of spiritual work wasn't enough, Anna is also a Co-Mason and was raised to the Sublime Degree of Master Mason in 2010.

Anna holds an M.A. degree in English Literature from Loyola University Chicago and she writes for fun and profit. She avidly blogs about her spiritual adventures at amoretmortem.wordpress.com.

Aside from writing, she expresses herself through Pagan jewelry and art, which she sells on her Etsy site, JackalMoonDesigns. She shares her home with two gloriously goofy rescue dogs, six slinky rescue cats, and the most beautiful of corn snakes.

www.ingramcontent.com/pod-product-compliance
Lightning Source LLC
Chambersburg PA
CBHW071942120726
48001CB00005B/2009